Straight Talk About Teen Dating

If I'd only known the truth about . . .

James Wegert M.Ed.

SOUTHWEST

This book is dedicated to my beloved Pam - without her love and support this book would not have been possible.

Table of Contents

Preface

"Why should I take the time to read this book? I'm busy!"

This book is like no other. It's going to give you a perspective on teen dating that you probably have never heard before. At times you may feel like yelling and tearing the book to pieces. **I urge you to hang in there and read it all the way to the end.** Please forgive me in advance for being overly blunt at times.

This book was written for you. Its purpose is to give you the information that you need before you start dating and also while you're dating.

Once again, my request is that you take the time to read the book from cover to cover, even if you don't agree with some of the information. If you decide to get married someday, hopefully this book will help you to have what Christ wants - a lifelong loving relationship with Him (Christ) and the best possible lifelong loving relationship with your husband or wife. The intent of the book is not to offend anyone - but just to give you the truth - usually short and to the point, sometimes not, but always the straight story with - "no baloney!"

This book wasn't designed to be read once and forgotten. It was designed to be referred back to over and over again - think of it as a handbook or a roadmap for dating. (Isn't it a good idea to have a map before you go down a road that you have never been on before or that you haven't been on long?)

Look around you, the quality of many relationships between men and women is poor. Many people do not have a loving marriage relationship. The divorce rate is skyrocketing and divorce is devastating this generation as well as damaging generations to come. We've got to take action in order to improve the quality of relationships and reduce the divorce rate

– we can't just have the "that's the way it is – there's nothing we can do about it" attitude. That attitude is "baloney." My hope is that this book will spark a cultural revolution as described in the Epilogue.

I'm going to share with you many things that I wish I'd known during my teenage years and early twenties. My hope is that the information contained in this book will help you to avoid some of the mistakes that I made.

I could have avoided so much heartache and mental anguish if I'd only known the truth about . . .

1

. . . the world having lots of very messed up people

As a teenager, I really didn't have a clue about what was going on in the world around me. I didn't know that the world has lots of very messed up people*. I mistakenly thought that almost all children were raised in a home like mine - a home in which they were given discipline as needed by parents who loved them. Little did I know that there were lots of parents who didn't really care about bringing up their children right or who didn't have the parenting skills and / or the strength needed to bring up their children right. (In other words, there are many people out in the world that have significant problems because of how they were brought up.)

When parents don't fulfill their responsibilities, it has a negative effect upon their children and on generations to come. Unfortunately, children who are not raised right (those who never learn integrity, honestly, concern and respect for others, what real love is, selflessness, and the importance of hard work) usually don't know how to raise their children right and the cycle continues to the next generation.

Violence, greed, selfishness, drug and alcohol abuse, premarital sex, having children out of wedlock, divorce - all of these things in our society today could be significantly reduced if parents would do a better job of fulfilling their responsibilities.

A number of months ago, just a few miles north of where I live, an eighteen-year-old man shot a mother and a father to death after they confronted him about being out all night with their fourteen-year-old daughter. You might be saying to yourself "What does that have to do with me?" This is just one example of the evil going on in our world. Look all around you; it is filled with horrible things like violence, lust, greed, drinking, drugs, and selfishness.

You need to know that many people are very messed up (mentally, emotionally, spiritually) because you are about to leave the protective cocoon of your family and go out into the world. It is very important for your sake that you do not end up marrying a person who is very messed up. (If you do, your life could become a living Hell.)

The truth is - you are about to go to war - you need strength from God and good information in order to have the best possible life here on earth.

(*Not to insult you, but unfortunately all of us are messed up mentally, emotionally, and / or spiritually to some degree. After all, we are human.)

2

. . . the war zone all around us

As a teenager I didn't realize that we are all living in a war zone. Yeah, I know it sounds crazy, like I'm out of my mind, - but I'm completely serious. And the war zone today is even more dangerous now than it was then.

This war zone I'm talking about isn't like the one you see on TV or on the news with guys shooting at each other - it is a war zone in your heart and mind between the forces of good and the forces of evil. (I know it still sounds a bit wacko, but hear me out.)

It's crucial that you understand that you are being bombarded by evil influences that want to control your heart and mind. For example, the content of many magazines, movies, TV shows, and music is not pleasing to God. They glamorize filthy language, alcohol / drug use, violence, lust, and sex outside of marriage. I realize that they may be exciting to read, watch or listen to for the moment, but you need to know that they damage your heart and mind. This is especially true for males who watch or see filth, because they can visualize what they have seen for a long, long time - it is almost as if it was burned permanently into their brain.

Sadly, if I want to, I can still visualize one of the first pornographic pictures that I was shown by a "friend" when I was in fifth or sixth grade. So don't believe anyone who says,

"Yeah, I look at, watch, and listen to that stuff - but it doesn't have any effect on me." They are fooling themselves - "no baloney!"

The truth is that God doesn't want you to fill up your head with garbage. You need to know that the reason so much garbage is being produced by the media is because garbage sells. Do you understand that many people are trying to put garbage into your head in order to make a buck? In other words, they are taking advantage of you for their own personal gain. They know that the value systems of many young people are not solidly formed. They are trying to impose their evil value system upon you, they want you to embrace evil, - so that they can sell you more garbage in the future! They could care less about you as a person and the negative effect that watching or listening to their garbage has upon your heart and mind.

With so many parents not fulfilling their responsibilities and the amount of garbage put out by the media on a daily basis - is it any surprise that filthy language, alcohol / drug use, violence, sex outside of marriage is widespread in our society?

3

. . . divorce devastating our society

I didn't think much about divorce when I was your age. It seemed to hardly ever happen and when it did it, it wasn't talked about. Man, have times changed - for the worse. Everywhere you go and in the media you hear about people getting divorced. The soaring divorce rate proves that the quality of relationships between husband and wife are at an all time low. Count your blessings if you have not been directly affected by divorce in some manner. Divorce, something that used to be almost unheard of, is now commonplace. It's almost accepted as something that "just happens."

Well, you need to know that it doesn't "just happen" - as you will see in this book, most divorces could be avoided: 1. if people were spiritually, emotionally, and financially ready before they started dating 2. if people knew what real love was 3. if people consulted God before deciding who to date and who to marry 4. if people grew up and learned how to give unselfish love.

Without a doubt, divorce leaves a path of destruction that not only damages or devastates adults; it also damages or devastates their children and you guessed it, future generations. More and more children are growing up without a Mom or a Dad sometime during their childhood. The family, the fabric that holds our society together, is crumbling. (Some people say that our society couldn't possibly crumble and fall - isn't that exactly what many nations that no longer exist thought?) Don't listen to the "baloney" that you may hear in the media about a "good divorce" – all divorces have negative effects upon people and their families.

Quite frankly, drastic action needs to be taken to attack this problem that threatens our society and it needs to be taken quickly. **We need to have a cultural revolution!** (Details of this revolution are described in the Epilogue of this book.)

4

. . . the two main values in our society

As a teenager I never heard anyone talk about what the two main values were in society. If they did, I wasn't paying attention.

I'm not sure where, but I heard or read somewhere that the two main values in our society today are personal gain and personal pleasure. Think about it, aren't they the two things that most people are concerned about? - people want to get as much as they can (money, possessions, etc.) and they want as much pleasure as possible (drinking, sex outside of marriage, drugs, gambling, you name it). You need to know that many people have been brainwashed by the media and their "friends" into thinking that personal gain and personal pleasure - in other words selfishness - is the way to happiness. I mean after all, if it feels good do it, right? - Not (more on the topic of selfishness in Chapter 26).

Keep in mind that what God values is usually the opposite of what man values. The Bible says that the two greatest commandments are "Love the Lord God with all your heart, mind, strength and soul" and "Love others as you love yourself" - which means to be just as concerned about the needs of others as we're concerned about our own needs. (We're concerned about having food in our stomach, clothes on our back, a roof over our heads, etc. God wants us to be just as concerned about others having their basic needs met.) So our focus in life is supposed to be upon loving God and loving others.

Do you see how far away what our society values is from what our loving heavenly Father values? It's like night and day.

5

. . . the importance of becoming a Christian

This chapter is not meant to insult anyone but at the same time I've got to be faithful to my Father in Heaven and I've got to keep my promise to you in the preface of "no baloney!" I am going to go into more detail in this chapter than others because **becoming a Christian is without question the most important decision that a person can make in his or her life.**

You may have had a reaction when you read the last sentence. You may have said out loud or to yourself something like "That's baloney!" - or something worse. You may have thrown down this book. I can understand your reaction especially if you are not being raised by parents who love Christ. My request to you is that you keep reading with as open a mind as possible. I want you to take the time to find out if being a Christian is "baloney" or if Jesus Christ told the truth when He said that whosoever believes in Him will have eternal life. You owe it to yourself to take the time to find out if Christianity is the truth or if it is a lie.*

My Pastor, in one of his sermons, said that "Christianity is inclusive, not exclusive." This means that anyone who wants to, regardless of what they have done in their life, can become a Christian. God will forgive you for whatever you've done if you turn to him and decide to trust in Christ alone as your Savior.

God promises eternal life to anyone who trusts in Christ alone as his or her Savior - it is a free gift from God, it cannot be earned, and there are no other requirements - "no baloney!"

So, what is a Savior anyway? A Savior is someone who saves someone from something horrible.

You may be asking the question, "Why do I need a Savior, someone to save me - I haven't done anything really bad in my life?" The reason is that God is perfect and he doesn't let anyone who is not perfect into heaven. Do you know anyone who is perfect in thought, word, and deed? I don't, including myself. That means that we are all sinners and the Bible says that we deserve to die because of our sins. (I know this sounds harsh - but that's what the Bible says)

And this death I'm talking about isn't just the death of your body. I'm talking about death as in being punished forever in Hell. Many people don't believe that Hell exists and many people don't believe that Hell is a place of eternal torment. Very sadly, they are wrong. Why do you think that the Bible, the handbook for living that God gave to us, mentions Hell numerous times and warns us to take whatever action is necessary to avoid being thrown into Hell? The reason is that Hell is a real place, and since God loves us, He doesn't want us to end up there.

The Good News is that God loves us so much that he sent his only Son to live on this earth over 2000 years ago and to die in our place on the cross. I realize that someone dying in your place is kind of hard to understand - so let me back up in time. In the years before Jesus Christ lived, people brought animals and grain to be sacrificed on the altar at the Temple in order for their sins to be forgiven. Simply stated, the animals and / or grain were placed on the altar and the High Priest said a prayer asking God to transfer the sins of the people to the animals / grain.

Then the fire consumed the sacrifice and the sins of the people were forgiven. It was as if their sins never existed. So Jesus dying on the cross for you and for me was the sacrifice of all sacrifices. Why? - because He was perfect - He was and is the Son of God. He died on the cross as a sacrifice for the sins that you have committed so far in your life - and amazingly for the sins that you will commit today as well as during the rest of your life here on earth. He will only be this sacrifice for you if you decide to believe in Him and receive the gift of eternal life. In other words, you will live forever with God if you make the decision to trust in Christ alone as your Savior.

You may be asking, "I'm confused about what it means to trust in Christ alone as your Savior." I know it's hard to relate to something that happened over 2000 years ago. Perhaps this story will help - let's imagine that your life is like driving an 18-wheel truck for the first time, with no training. At times you think you have things under control, things seem to be going pretty well, but truth be told you don't really know what you're doing. Probably sometime during your life you are going to have a crash, it might be a crash from a drinking problem, it may be a crash from a divorce, it may be a crash from losing your job, or from something else.

So for the sake of moving this story along, let's say that your life does crash - in fact you crash your 18-wheel truck on a highway bridge, you know one of those bridges that goes over another highway. Your truck is lying on its side against the

guardrail of that bridge and you are hanging from the cab door
that opened from the impact of the wreck. You are looking
down at solid concrete 100 feet below. Just then the engine
bursts into flames. You're in deep trouble. You don't know what
you are going to do.

It just so happens that a taxi is driving on the road underneath
the bridge. The taxi driver looks up and sees you hanging from
the cab door. He pulls his taxi off the road, jumps out, and runs
into the middle of the road just below you. He knows that you
are about to die. He decides that he is going to try to catch you.
He yells up to you "Let go - I'll catch you!"

You have a choice, you can either hold on to the cab door and
be burned or you can trust that the Taxi Driver will catch you.
Because the flames are coming closer and closer to you, and the
Taxi Driver looks like he might be able to catch you, you decide
to let go. You are falling, tumbling, falling - the Taxi Driver
catches you, but your full weight crushes him. You escape with
only bumps and bruises. The Taxi Driver who broke your fall
has massive internal injuries and broken bones from your
weight.

How would you feel about the Taxi Driver after he did this for
you? Please think about it for a few seconds. . . . . . I bet you
would have some tender feelings toward him in your heart,
feelings of gratitude, feelings of compassion, maybe even
feelings of brotherly love. And I'm sure that you would visit
him in the hospital. And you are there - the Taxi Driver isn't
doing very well. He's in bad shape; the Doctor's haven't been
able to stop the internal bleeding. He notices you out of the
corner of his eye. You smile and ask how he's doing. He
motions for you to come over. You walk over, bend down, and

he whispers in your ear, "I want you to trust in Christ alone as your Savior and I want you to love other people" - then he closes his eyes and dies.

I bet that you would remember those words the rest of your life. I bet that you would trust in Christ alone as your Savior and that you would do your best to love other people.

So who does the Taxi Driver in the story represent? . . . That's right, the Taxi Driver represents Jesus Christ. We all have a choice in our life, we can hold onto our life and live our life selfishly without God . . . and be tormented in Hell forever. Or we can let go, and trust in Christ alone to save us – and then try our best to live our life the way God wants us to. Just as the Taxi Driver died in your place in the story, Jesus Christ died in your place 2000 years ago on the cross. Remember the tender feelings you had toward the Taxi Driver after he saved you? Do you have the same tender feelings toward Jesus Christ? Do you realize how much God truly loves you just the way you are? Do you realize that God wants you to trust in Christ alone as your Savior and that he wants you to love others?

You may be asking, "Is there anything else that you can tell me to explain what trusting in Christ alone as my Savior means?" Maybe this example will help: Imagine yourself sitting on a folding chair with your feet tucked under the chair so that no part of your body is touching the floor. At that point you are trusting in the chair alone to keep you from falling to the ground. Many people trust in a lot of things to try to earn their way to heaven - being a good person, doing good deeds, going to church, giving money to the church, etc. The problem is that being in heaven when your body dies can't be earned - it is a gift from God. In this example the chair represents Jesus Christ

13

- if you trust in Christ alone as your Savior you will be with God forever.

The most important question of all is: Do you know if you die today that you will be in heaven? It's great if you have made the decision to accept the gift of eternal life from God by trusting in Christ alone as your Savior. If not, my prayer is that very soon you will get down on your knees and pray a prayer in your own words something like this: "Father in heaven, I admit that I have sinned many times in my life, please forgive me for my sins both in the past and in the future. I accept your gift of eternal life by placing all of my trust for getting to heaven in what Christ did on the cross for me. I am trusting in Christ alone as my Savior. Help me to have a close relationship with you and to live my life in a way that would be pleasing to you. Amen."

If you have decided to trust in Christ alone as your Savior, God has sent his Holy Spirit to dwell inside of you - that's right God is inside! - how awesome is that!! (see John , chapter 14, verse 16). You will never be alone even if everyone here on earth abandons you. God will help you through whatever problems you have in your life. He doesn't promise us a problem free life, but he promises that he will help us through anything.

(*Many people throughout history have questioned whether or not the Bible is true and whether or not Christ actually died on the cross for our sins. Remember that no important fact from the Bible has ever been proven wrong. The greatest evidence that the Bible is true is the fact that hundreds of millions of peoples' lives have been changed for the good after they trusted in Christ alone as their Savior.)

6

. . . the Christian lifestyle being the most exciting of all

Before I became a Christian, I used to think that the Christian lifestyle was boring. You know - being "good" and reading the Bible all the time.

The truth is that if you are living your life for Christ, the Christian lifestyle is the most exciting of all. For example:

There's something special about living your life for the creator and ruler of the entire universe

There's something special about being able to confess your sins in prayer and have them forgiven instantly

There's something special about being able to put your head on the pillow each night knowing that you are in His loving embrace and that He loves you more than you can imagine

There's something special about Him helping you to be loving, happy, peaceful, patient, kind, gentle, self-controlled, faithful, and good (see Galatians, chapter 5, verses 22-23)

There's something special about having a Christian wife who loves the Lord

There's something special about fellowship with Christian friends - friends who will help you in times of trouble and who will celebrate with you in times of joy

There's something special about knowing that Christ is always with you throughout the ups and downs of life (As a Christian, I know in my heart that together, He and I, we will make it through this life here on earth. And after my earthly life is over, he will keep his promise and I will live with Him forever. I'm getting goose bumps just writing this. Please see Matthew, Chapter 28, verse 20.)

Living your life for yourself pales in comparison to living your life for Christ - "no baloney!"

(Just wanted to share a story to give you a little example of the Christian lifestyle being the most exciting on earth: When we lived in a small town in Virginia, our Pastor accepted a new position at a large church in Chicago. The church decided to give him a grand sendoff party - and grand it was. In the banquet room of Ernie's restaurant, one group after another from the church performed a humorous skit or song honoring the Pastor. We almost couldn't stop laughing.

The presentation by the Senior Citizens was the high point of the evening. The Pastor rode a Harley, so about six Senior ladies dressed up in full length leather motorcycle outfits and sang on stage the song "The Leader of the Pack." The laughter was almost deafening. At one point during the evening, the Pastor stood on his chair waving his napkin in a big circle above his head with the music blaring to pump up the crowd. I noticed that the restaurant employees standing off to the side were wide eyed and amazed about what was going on. Here was a church group, without any alcohol, almost raising the roof off the place. I think that our church did a great job that night of showing that the Christian lifestyle is the most exciting on earth.)

James Wegert

7

. . . God doesn't want everyone to be married

I can almost hear you saying, "What? Are you kidding me?" In the Bible, the Apostle Paul says in 1 Corinthians, chapter 7, verse 8 that it's perfectly OK not to be married. (A married person is concerned about pleasing his or her spouse and family – and that can make him or her less concerned with pleasing God.)

In 1 Corinthians, chapter 7, verse 9, Paul also says that it is better for a person to get married than it is to burn with lust.

James Wegert

.

8

. . . dating not being around very long

I used to think that dating had pretty much been around forever. Then I found out that dating is relatively recent in history - it's only been around for a couple of hundred years at the most.

Dating is something that was started by man and just like most things started by man - it has many flaws. For example: Flaw #1: People are being encouraged by society to date at a younger and younger age. Peer pressure (which is just an evil influence in the war to win your heart and mind) tells you that something is wrong with you if you don't have a boyfriend or a girlfriend at an early age. Flaw #2: Most people that date are not spiritually, emotionally, and / or financially ready to date. Flaw #3: Most people who date don't have the information that they need before they start dating, they don't know who to date and how to date - so many people end up marrying the wrong person - which often leads to divorce.

(One of the goals of this book is to give you the information that you need in order to date well.)

James Wegert

9

. . . why dating is so important to people

Think about it - we humans do both positive and negative things to try to feel good about ourselves. We all want to gain status in the eyes of others - we all want to be somebody. People try to feel good about themselves in many different ways: by being good at a sport, by playing an instrument well, by winning a game, by rooting for a winning team, by being a good person, by being an excellent student, by using alcohol and other drugs, by winning a fight with someone else, by buying as much "stuff" as possible, by gambling - the list goes on and on.

If you polled teenagers about why they want to date you might get responses like: "I really like him", "I really like her", "he's really exciting", "she's hot", "he's cute", "most of my friends are dating", among others.

I don't think that many teenagers will come up with the real reason if you ask them. May I suggest that the reason most teenagers want to date is that they want to feel good about themselves and / or they want to feel loved. After all it's only human nature - we want to feel important, we want to have someone who really cares about us, we want to be respected by our peers, and we want to feel attractive to the opposite sex. Being in a dating relationship usually helps us to feel good about ourselves.

The problem is that our feeling good about ourselves and feeling loved isn't supposed to come from being in a dating relationship - and it's not supposed to come from any of the other things people do that were mentioned at the beginning of this chapter.

Our unshakable feeling good about ourselves is supposed to come from having a close relationship with Jesus Christ. If we have trusted in Christ alone as our Savior, we are now a child of God forever, he loves us endlessly, and we will live with Him eternally - wow are those ever good reasons to feel good about yourself! Becoming a Christian and living a Christian life is the only lasting way for a person to feel good about himself or herself - "no baloney!"

10

. . . the world teaching us that early dating is OK

(This chapter is going to sound like I am hammering on parents and grandparents - that is not my intent; I know they have a tough job. I hope that the words that I have written will help them to take a stand against early dating if they haven't already - and that they will help you to take a stand if you become a parent someday.)

Yesterday my six-year-old told me proudly "I have eight girlfriends." It was an innocent comment that sheds light on what the world teaches us about dating. The world teaches us that dating at an early age is "normal", "acceptable", "a good thing", or "cute". Obviously we learn it at an early age. You've probably heard a parent or a grandparent proudly say with a smile something like "Suzie is twelve and she already has a boyfriend" or "Billy is fifteen, he's dating, in fact he's had three girlfriends already."

When I hear something like this, I feel a bit sick to my stomach and I feel like saying: 1. "Why are you allowing your child or grandchild to date - don't you realize that your child or grandchild is not spiritually or emotionally ready to date?" 2. "Don't you realize that young people who date at an early age are much more likely to have premarital sex and be infected with a sexually transmitted disease?" 3. "Don't you realize that young people who date at an early age usually follow the pattern of becoming emotionally attached, going steady, and then breaking up?" (The problem is that soon after their breakup they usually start the pattern all over again with someone else. They are damaging their emotions and they are developing a dangerous pattern that all too often happens again in marriage. They repeat the pattern by dating, getting engaged, getting married, and getting divorced. Breaking the emotional attachment of marriage becomes way too easy because they have broken an emotional attachment many times before. Think about it.)

So why do parents or grandparents not take a stand against early dating? May I suggest that perhaps they dated early themselves (and it worked out fine) and that they too have been influenced by the media and their friends to think that early dating is OK. Parents and grandparents need to teach their children at a young age about the dangers of early dating. They need to have the backbone to say "no" and avoid copout statements like "boys will be boys" and "girls will be girls."

Parents and grandparents need to: 1. understand that their child or grandchild is constantly being bombarded with media messages as well as peer pressure that encourage early dating and early sexuality 2. do whatever needs to be done to help their child resist peer pressure and break through the garbage put out daily by the media 3. understand that the media wants their child's heart and mind so that they can make as much money as possible 4. explain to their children or grandchildren that the way God wants them to live their life compared to the way the media and their "friends" tell them how to live their life, is often exactly the opposite of each other 5. have a close loving relationship with their child and give them guidance about life on a daily basis 6. spend time everyday listening to and talking with their child 7. make sure that their child reads and understands the parts of the Bible that pertain to daily living and love (for example - Proverbs, Romans, Ephesians, and 1 Corinthians) 8. make it very clear that the reason God gave us the Bible, our handbook for living life, is that He loves us and that He wants only the very best for us.

James Wegert

11

. . . dating at an early age usually is a big mistake

(Much of this material was mentioned in the last chapter - but it's so important it's worth repeating.)

Based upon what I've read, statistics show that the earlier a young person starts to date . . .

. . . the more likely they will have premarital sex

. . . the more likely they will be infected with one or more sexually transmitted diseases

. . . the more likely they will become a parent without being married

. . . the more likely they will be divorced in their lifetime

One of the biggest dangers of starting to date at an early age is that young people get into the pattern of dating, going steady, becoming emotionally attached, and then breaking up - for many people this happens over and over again during the teenage years. They get into a pattern of being emotionally attached to another person and then tearing that attachment apart when they don't "feel like" being attached anymore.

Sadly, many people repeat this pattern by dating, getting engaged, getting married, and when they don't "feel like" being attached anymore - getting divorced.

12

. . . the importance of first developing your relationship with Jesus Christ

Millions of teens are making the mistake of spending a lot of their precious time developing relationships with people of the opposite sex (please keep in mind that just because millions of teens are making this mistake - it doesn't mean that you should just go along with the crowd). The media (music, magazines, TV, movies) constantly emphasizes how important these relationships are. The fact is that a human relationship should never ever be your most important relationship - your most important relationship should be the one with Jesus Christ. It is absolutely essential to develop a close relationship with your Savior before you even think about developing a relationship with a boyfriend or girlfriend - "no baloney!"

You may be asking how in the world do I go about developing a close relationship with Jesus Christ? First of all you need to become a Christian as was explained in Chapter 5.

Next, you need to set aside time everyday to develop your relationship with Him. I can almost hear you saying, "I haven't got time for that - I've got too many things that I have to get done, too many things that I want to do." A lesson that I have learned from school and work is that I am most effective when I make it a point to always work first on the highest priority thing that I need to do. I know it's going to be tough, but you need to

31

make spending time developing your relationship with Jesus Christ your highest priority.

Here's some reasons why:

- Because Jesus said that the greatest commandment was "to love the Lord your God with all you heart, mind, strength, and soul" (if we love God, we are supposed to obey him)

- Because having a close relationship with Jesus Christ will help you to make good decisions in life and it will help you to make it through the tough times in life (Hebrews, chapter 13, verse 5 says that the Lord has promised that He will never leave or abandon us)

- Because having a close relationship with Jesus Christ will help you to have a much better life here on earth and it will prepare you to live with God forever

Here's more suggestions of how to go about developing your relationship with Him: 1. Get yourself a good Bible that is written for teens. 2. Read it every other day at the least - start out in John and move to other books that talk about daily living and love - such as Proverbs, Romans, 1 Corinthians, Ephesians, etc. 3. Spend time in prayer daily including praising God; thanking God for all of your blessings; confessing your sins of thought, word, or deed; asking God to forgive your sins; asking God for help forgiving other people; asking God for wisdom to make good decisions that are pleasing to him; asking God for strength to live your life each day the way he wants you to; sharing things with him that are bothering or worrying you; and praying for other people (for example - friends, relatives, unsaved people, people who you don't get along with). It will also be helpful to use some of your prayer time to be silent and listen to God. 4. If you're not already, start listening to your choice of Christian music instead of music about relationships between a man and a woman - there's some good Christian music out there and it can help you to have a closer relationship with Jesus Christ.

Here's a suggested list of priorities in life: #1 - your daily time in prayer, #2 - your time reading the Bible (at least every other day), #3 - eating, #4 - sleeping, #5 - your time with your family, #6 - exercise (three times a week), #7 - your school work, #8 - your time with strong Christian friends (see Chapter 18), #9 - everything else.

Doesn't it make sense to spend a large amount of time in your younger years building the foundation of your life on the rock, Jesus Christ, by developing a close relationship with Him - instead of wasting too much of your time developing human relationships (dating) that will more than likely not result in a lifelong loving Christian marriage? Please see Matthew, chapter 7, verses 24-27.

James Wegert

13

. . . the importance of being a FDFOC before dating

The Bible makes it very clear in 2 Corinthians, chapter 6, verse 14 that we are not to be yoked (attached) with unbelievers. So, in other words, God does not want a Christian to marry someone who is not a Christian. So how do you do your best to prevent that from happening? Here are two suggestions:

- Do whatever it takes to become a fully devoted follower of Christ* (FDFOC) before you start dating (discussed in this chapter)

- Do whatever it takes to only date another fully devoted follower of Christ (discussed in the next chapter)

You need to understand that if you have decided to trust in Christ alone as your Savior, you are now a child of God and he loves you dearly. You are a jewel to him and he only wants the best for you. He wants you to have the best possible life here on earth and when he decides that your physical body is going to die, he will take you to Heaven and you will live with Him forever. (What a wonderful thought, think about it)

As you grow in your relationship with Jesus Christ, you will eventually come to the point where you become fully devoted to Him . . . you feel strongly that your relationship with Him is at the center of your life, you want to spend time with Him everyday to grow that relationship, you love Him dearly, and you have decided to put Him in charge of your life instead of yourself. This process of becoming a fully devoted follower of Christ takes time . . . years and years. After all, how can you tell if you are really fully devoted to Christ unless that devotion has stood the test of time during the ups and downs of life?

So, don't even think about dating until you are sure that you are a fully devoted follower of Christ. If you are a girl and someone asks you out, tell them, "Sorry, but I have decided not to date at this time." You probably will be ridiculed by others, but shouldn't you be more concerned with pleasing God than you are with pleasing humans? If you're a guy, forget about asking someone out until you are a fully devoted follower of Christ. Ask God in prayer to give you strength to stand up against the peer pressure to date. (I realize that peer pressure seems overwhelming, but even more overwhelming is the power of God if you tap into it through daily prayer - ask Him for strength. Christian friends can also help you to be strong - see Chapter 18.)

Being a fully devoted follower of Christ and marrying a fully devoted follower of Christ (see Chapter 14) means that you have built your house (your marriage) on a foundation of rock - Jesus Christ. That means that when the storms of life come - in the form of problems, conflict, and possibly even tragedy - your marriage will be much more likely to survive the storm. Another way to think about it is when the going gets tough, strong Christian faith is the glue that helps to hold couples together. Ecclesiastes, chapter 4, verse 12 says that "A rope made from three strands of cord is hard to break." The three strands are God, man, and woman.

(*I first heard this expression at the church I attend. I take no credit.)

James Wegert

14

. . . the importance of only dating a FDFOC

Not many people are interested in holding a stick of dynamite that has just been lit. This is exactly what you are doing if you decide to date someone who is not a FDFOC. It's too easy to become emotionally attached to someone who says they are a Christian, but who is not a fully devoted follower of Christ. No matter how nice, how cute, how beautiful - please don't do it.

I know it sounds black and white, you might even be saying to yourself "what could one date hurt?", but I need to warn you about the possible consequences. You need to realize that you are setting yourself up to become emotionally attached to someone who God does not want you to marry. You are setting yourself up for misery and heartbreak. Unfortunately I know - I made this mistake.

Here's my painful story: I met a young lady at a fraternity (one with a Christian emphasis) party during my senior year of college. She was beautiful on the outside (the dangers of which are described in Chapter 17). We talked for about two hours, we seemed to have some things in common, and I ended up walking her back to her dorm. We had many dates, she said that she was a Christian, and we went to church together just about every week while we were dating. We dated for about two years before we married. After almost nine years of marriage, she told me that she wanted to do "her own thing" and she moved out. On the day of the divorce hearing, just over ten years from when we were married, the judge asked her why she was seeking a divorce. She didn't have a reason. It was not until years later that I realized the two big mistakes that I had made - I dated when I was not yet a fully devoted follower of Christ and I dated a person that was not a fully devoted follower of Christ.

My prayer is that this book will help you to avoid the mistake that I made.

(The good news is that with God's help I didn't make the same mistake twice. He has blessed me with a sweet wife who is a fully devoted follower of Christ and two precious sons.)

15

. . . how to recognize a FDFOC

It's crucial to be able to recognize a fully devoted follower of Christ. Here's a little bit of a checklist that may help you (beware that many people who say they are fully devoted followers of Christ - are not):

1. They freely tell others that they are a Christian

2. They have been a Christian and have been living a Christian lifestyle for several years (the longer the better).

3. They continuously seek God's will for their life - they ask for God's guidance and help in every important decision

4. They recognize and accept God's authority over them - their behavior reflects this fact

5. They take responsibility for their actions. They ask for forgiveness as needed

6. They read their Bible on a regular basis

7. They know and obey God's word

8. They spend time in daily prayer

9. The most important relationship in their life is their

relationship with Jesus Christ

10. They have a close relationship with Him

11. Their desire is to deepen (grow) their relationship with Jesus Christ

12. They feel good about themselves based upon their position as a child of God

13. They display the fruits of the Holy Spirit - love, joy, peace, patience, kindness, goodness, faithfulness, gentleness, and self-control

14. They treat everyone with kindness and respect - even people who are disrespected by other people

15. They have empathy and compassion for others

16. They willingly forgive other people

17. They are a giving person, not a selfish person

16

. . . the importance of emotional / financial maturity

The last three chapters talked about the importance of spiritual maturity - being a FDFOC and dating only a FDFOC. Before you date, you also need to consider emotional and financial maturity.

Unfortunately, many people are not emotionally mature enough to start dating (they, of course, will tell you otherwise). Some people are emotionally needy - they need to have a relationship with someone to help them feel good about themselves. You need to be aware of the dangers of dating this type of person. They become emotionally attached very quickly and demand a lot of attention - they tend to suffocate you with their needs. Many people who are not emotionally mature are selfish. You do not want to date and marry a selfish person. (Selfishness is discussed in more detail in Chapter 26.)

You will see in Chapter 27 that problems controlling money is one of the five main causes of divorce. Many people have never been taught by their parents how to control money. They earn or are given money, but it goes through their fingers very quickly without much to show for it. It is very important that at least one person in a marriage have the capability to earn what is needed to support the family and that both people know how to spend money wisely. I encourage you to read books about how to control your money using a budget that includes saving for the future. (Please see the Appendix of this book for more information about a Teen U™ course designed to help you learn how to control your money.)

In the ideal world, it would be great if people would enter into a dating relationship only if they are both fully devoted followers of Christ and only after they have a few years of work experience (after their education) under their belt. This is when it is more likely that a person will have the emotional and financial maturity needed to start dating.

It's almost like concrete - when you first graduate from high school, college or technical school and start a full-time job, the concrete for the foundation of your building (your life) has just been poured. It takes a few years for that concrete to fully harden, to be at its full strength. It's not good to join two buildings together when one or both of the buildings have weak concrete. The possibility of collapse (divorce) is higher.

17

. . . the danger of being too concerned with beauty on the outside

Our society and the media are completely caught up in beauty on the outside. Just look at the magazines, TV, and the movies. Men especially are attracted visually. When we get caught up in beauty on the outside, our brains tend to stop working. We ignore obvious character flaws because we are so enamored that they are "beautiful" or "cute". Millions and millions of people have fallen into this trap - including me.

The key thing that we all need to remember is that beauty on the outside eventually fades, but beauty on the inside lasts forever. If God wants you to be married, he wants you to marry someone who is beautiful on the inside - a person who displays the fruits of the Spirit (listed in #13 on p. 42) everyday. It's a joy to spend each day with such a person.

You will need to learn how to look for beauty on the inside if and when you start to date. Please see Chapter 15 about how to identify a person with beauty on the inside - a fully devoted follower of Christ.

James Wegert

18

. . . the importance of Christian friends

You may be asking, "Why are Christian friends so important?"
The reason is that we were not meant to go through this life
alone. You need to find a group of Christian friends to be a part
of at your church, school, or both. You need to be part of a
group with teens who are interested in learning how to live their
lives for Christ.

Christian friends will talk with you, encourage you, and help
you through the downs of life. They will celebrate with you
during the ups of life, help you to have a closer relationship
with Jesus Christ, help you to stay focused on living your life
daily for Him, help you resist negative peer pressure, give you
wise counsel when needed (in other words, tell you what you
need to hear even when you don't want to hear it). They will
truly be your friends forever.

A parent of a teen recently told me that their teen wants to "fit
in" with her peers. Unfortunately, often this desire to "fit in"
and "be accepted" by peers causes teens to make bad decisions
- sometimes decisions that affect them for the rest of their lives.
Please really make an effort to find a group of Christian friends
with whom you can "fit in." (Your best bet is to find a church
youth group that has an adult leader who is a fully devoted
follower of Christ and participate in the group on a regular
basis.) It's not easy trying to live your life on this earth in a way
that is pleasing to Christ. We need help from our Christian

friends and from Christ Himself. Remember, Christ never promised us that our life on this earth would be easy - but He did promise us in Matthew, chapter 28, verse 20 that He would be with us "always." In other words, no matter how bad things get in life, Christ will help us through if we put our faith and trust in Him.

(Just a word of warning about spending too much time with friends that may not be outwardly evil, but who are not Christians - you tend to become more like the people you hang with, so if you spend a lot of time with people who don't think having a relationship with Jesus Christ is important, over time your relationship with Him will tend to become less important to you.)

Speaking of non-Christian friends, here's the true story about the first time I ever asked someone out on a date. I was a junior in High School, but I was only fifteen because I started school a year early. I had my eye on a beautiful "blonde bombshell" that was a junior varsity cheerleader. I just missed the deadline for the fall Driver's Education class, so I wasn't going to be able to drive until the spring semester. I wanted to ask this girl out on a date but I didn't want to have my Dad drive us and pick us up - I would be too embarrassed.

I told my "friend" Justin (name has been changed to protect the innocent) about my desire to ask her out on a date. He told me "I'll drive you if you get a date, but you don't have the guts to ask her." Well, he was wrong. I practiced my asking for a date speech at least 50 times. I planned when and where in the school I would talk to her. I thought I had it planned perfectly because I was going to ask her to go to an away basketball game - games at which junior varsity cheerleaders didn't cheer. She didn't know me from Adam, but for some reason - I didn't think that was going to be a problem.

My heart was pounding, my mouth was dry, and the time had come. I walked up along side her in the hall near the end of the school day, turned to her and blurted out – "Hi, my name is Jim, I was wondering if you would consider going with me to the basketball game at Euclid?" She said, "I can't because I have to cheer." Awkwardly, I said, "I thought you didn't cheer at away games." She said kindly, "It's the only away game that we're going to this year - maybe some other time." I didn't know what to say so I just said, "Thanks." My knees were shaking as I walked away. It took me about an hour to completely calm down. That night I told Justin that I had asked her for a date. His reaction was "What! - I never thought you'd do it!" I told him that I planned to ask her out again. He said, "Well if you do - I'm not driving you." That's when I knew he wasn't really my friend - he never really intended to drive me on a date.

I was so shy and embarrassed that even though I saw her in the hall periodically I never said another word to her. She probably thought that I was some kind of weirdo. In hindsight, it may have been a blessing because I was nowhere near spiritually / emotionally / financially ready to start dating.

(Please read 1 Samuel, chapter 18, verse 1 through chapter 20, verse 42. It will give you a good idea about what Christian friendship is supposed to be like.)

James Wegert

19

. . . the importance of getting to know someone (what to look for) and prayer before you start dating

As we discussed in Chapter 14, it is essential to find out if a person is a fully devoted follower of Christ before you start dating them. I met my wife-to-be in a young adult Sunday School class. This can be a great place to meet people who are fully devoted followers of Christ. (But be careful, many people in these classes are not fully devoted followers of Christ.)

We were just acquaintances for about a year. During this time I was observing all of the ladies in the class to see how they related to other people. My goal was to get to know the ladies as much as possible without dating. (I realize that this is easier for a man to do than it would be for a woman.) I tried to participate in the group activities (retreats, "Super Bowl" parties, service projects, etc.) so that I would have a chance to observe their behavior outside of Sunday School class.

I was looking for a person who displayed the fruits of the Holy Spirit. Pam showed them in the way that she related to everyone. She was upbeat and personable. I never heard her say an unkind word to anyone. She especially impressed me with the amount of time that she took talking with a mentally handicapped lady in the class. While most of the ladies ignored this person or tried to keep their conversations with her short, Pam struck up a conversation with her on a regular basis, asked her questions, and seemed genuinely interested in her as a person. Her kindness to this lady really attracted me to Pam.

I started to pray to God about who he wanted me to ask out on a date. Then I specifically asked God if he wanted me to ask Pam out. I asked God this question in prayer for about a month. I felt that he was leading me to ask her out and so I did one day after Sunday School class. She has been the biggest blessing of my life ever since that day and I will love her until the day I die. I thank God for her every night in my prayers.

20

. . . the do's and don'ts of dating – how to really get to know a person while dating (including danger signs to look out for)

Let's say the time has come - you are a fully devoted follower of Christ and you are about to go out with a fully devoted follower of Christ - and you are old enough for group or one-on-one dating. (Please see p. 79-80 for important age information.) Here's some suggestions for doing dating right:

Do:

- Participate in as wide of a variety of wholesome activities as possible

- Talk about a wide variety of subjects

- Try to find out if you have interests in common (having common interests and hobbies helps to hold a relationship together)

- Go to church with him or her

- Pray with him or her

- Find out if he or she has a strong set of Christian friends (If he or she is a loner, he or she may be looking for you to meet all of his or her needs - this can put a strain on any relationship.)

- Carefully observe his or her words and deeds - does he or she display the fruits of the Holy Spirit consistently?

- Observe if he or she takes responsibility for his or her actions

- Observe if he or she shows respect to all other people - pay special attention to how he or she treats others who are often not well treated by the world (people in low paying jobs, people with disabilities, etc.)

- Observe if he or she has compassion toward other people and animals (does he or she have a tender heart?)

- Ask yourself the question: Is his or her focus in life on serving God or is it on himself or herself?

- Observe if he or she is a selfish person - if so, this is a major danger flag (see Chapter 26)

- Carefully observe how he or she reacts when something goes wrong and when he or she doesn't get their way or what they want - this will help you to get an idea of what his or her domestic personality is like. I read in a book, I think by the late Pastor O. Dean Martin, that we have a social personality and a domestic personality. The social personality is the one that we usually display in public - you know the cheerful and positive one. The domestic personality is the one that we display when we aren't out in public, our guards are down, and we aren't putting on a face - it's more like the real us. The domestic personality is the one that you are going to have to live with on a regular basis if you decide to get married. After I was engaged to my first wife, she asked me if I would stay with her Mother and her for several weeks while her Father was out of town. A few weeks earlier they had an attempted break-in at their house and they didn't want to stay alone while he was away.

She was asking me to drive an hour and a half each way to work. When I hesitated, she said in not the nicest tone, "Oh, I knew you wouldn't do it!" Unfortunately, I didn't realize it at the time, but she had just revealed some of her domestic personality.

- Observe how he or she treats his or her parents and other relatives (a lack of love and respect toward his or her family is a major danger sign)

- Observe how his or her Father and Mother relate to each other (Does one dominate the other? - a danger sign, Do they treat each other with respect? Do they seem to have a warm loving relationship? - often patterns in the parent's marriage are repeated when the child gets married.)

- Observe if he or she is too concerned with what other people think about him or her - instead of being concerned about what God thinks

- Observe if he or she does the right thing in situations when doing the wrong thing could personally benefit him or her - you are looking for a person who will do what is right (what is pleasing to God) no matter what

- Ask him or her to gradually read all of the books from the courses of Teen U™ as well as the highly recommended books listed in the Appendix of this book and at www.TeenU.net. Read the books yourself at the same time and then talk about all of them over a period of months (a good idea is to read a chapter at a time and then talk about it). Ask each other questions like: what did you learn from the chapter?, what were the most important points to you?, etc. It's also a good idea to do the exercises found in some of the books together. (This is a possible group dating activity that may spark some interesting discussions.)

- Pray that Christ would be the head of your dating relationship

- Ask God on a regular basis if he wants you to continue the dating relationship

- After prayers asking Christ for wisdom and guidance, break off a dating relationship with a person to whom you know that God does not want you to be married. Do it in a kind but firm way. Don't be sucked into the trap of going back into the relationship because now you are all alone. Remember that Christ is with you always and that he can help you through anything. Ask Him for strength.

Don't:

- Let the thrill of someone treating you well and making you feel special cause you to ignore obvious character flaws

- Let the fact that the person you are dating has money or has the potential to earn a lot of money blind you to their character flaws (Too many people have found out the hard way that the saying "money doesn't buy happiness" is true.)

- Beware of the danger of infatuation (the feeling of being "head over heels in love" with someone that you don't really know that well) - a warning sign of infatuation is that you think about him or her all the time

- Become emotionally attached too quickly - take things nice and slow

- Rush into thinking about getting married - statistics I've read show that longer dating relationships are more likely to become lifelong marriage relationships - a suggestion is that you date for at least two years in order to really get to know the other person (have a chance to observe his or her behavior in all types of situations, talk about almost everything) - you want to be absolutely sure that this is the person that God wants you to marry

- Spend excessive amount of time alone with him or her (<u>No</u> time alone if you have not graduated from high school - please see pages 79-80.)

- Spend much time kissing

- Touch another person's body anywhere that would not be pleasing to God (I heard somewhere - don't let yourself become aroused more than can be satisfied in a manner pleasing to God) - save God's gift of sexuality for the man or woman He wants you to marry

- Lay down together - I know that this may sound ridiculous and old fashioned, but keeping your feet on the floor is a good idea to help prevent things from getting out of hand.

- Drink alcohol - it definitely impairs your God given judgment

- Tell him or her that you love him or her until you fully understand what that means (please see the next chapter for details)

21

. . . what real love is

Unfortunately, most people don't know what real love is and that's the main reason why so many relationships between men and women are messed up. Most people think that real love is only a feeling. You know, the "I'm in love and it's wonderful" feeling.

If real love is only a feeling, feelings come and go. But real love doesn't come and go according to the Bible. A paraphrase of 1 Corinthians, chapter 13 is: Love is patient and kind. Love isn't jealous, rude, selfish, or easily angered. Love keeps no record of wrongs. Love finds no joy in evil, but rejoices in what is right. Love is supportive, loyal, hopeful, and trusting. **Love never fails.**

Real love is a commitment. When you say that you love someone, you are committing to loving them for the rest of your life - for richer, for poorer, in sickness and in health, from this day forward, until death do you part.

So when you hear someone say "I don't love him or her anymore" - take it for what it really is - an emotionally and / or spiritually immature person telling you that they never had real love for the person they are talking about to begin with - "no baloney!"

Over and over again I've heard young women say "my

boyfriend loves me." Unfortunately, most of these women have
been fooled. How could their boyfriend possibly love them
if their boyfriend doesn't even know what real love is?

How would you feel if you gave something of very high value
in exchange for something that you thought had a very high
value - and you later found out that what you received was
counterfeit? Angry? Betrayed? Outraged? Depressed? How do
you think millions of unmarried teenage girls feel after they find
out that they have given their precious virginity (commanded by
God to only be given to their husband) to someone who doesn't
really love them?**

It's time for young women to rise up and refuse to accept this
counterfeit love from these young men who are not fully
devoted followers of Christ. Young women need to realize that
many men who are not fully devoted followers of Christ view
women as sex objects - something to be used for their sexual
gratification. I'm sorry if this sounds insulting - but it's time for
many young women to wake up, wise up, and not be fooled. It's
time for teenage women to use their teenage years to develop a
close relationship with Jesus Christ instead of spending too
much precious time developing relationships with young men.

(It's also time for teenage men to use their teenage years to
develop a close relationship with Jesus Christ instead of
spending too much precious time developing relationships with
young women.)

**Please keep in mind that if you have given your virginity
away without being married - God still loves you deeply, he
forgives all things, and he will never turn his back on you -
please carefully consider becoming a Christian, if you're not

already, by trusting in Christ alone as your Savior and start living your life for Him! (Please see Chapter 5 and Chapter 12 for more information.)

22

. . . the danger of saying or hearing the words "I love you"

I heard those words "I love you" about two months after I started dating my first wife. I didn't know it at the time, but my first reaction was the right reaction, I said something like "It's only been a few months; you can't know that you love someone after two months."

But it didn't take long for my head to start swimming - in fact as I walked back to my college dorm I jumped up in the air and said, "She loves me!" Instead of seeing someone telling me that they loved me after two months as a danger sign, I was on cloud nine. I had swallowed it hook, line, and sinker and I was starting to feel "in love" myself. In fact I made the mistake of telling her that I loved her after about five months of dating. Unfortunately, her definition of love and my definition of love were not the same - and she ended what was supposed to be a lifelong loving Christian marriage relationship by divorcing me after ten years.

So I beg you, before you say those words - understand what they really are supposed to mean as explained in Chapter 21. Don't say them unless you really mean them - unless you are willing to make a lifelong commitment to the person that you are saying them to.

Also, be very wary of anyone who says these words to you who has been dating you for less than a year. Ask them what they mean when they say "I love you" and share what the words mean to you.

Don't fall into the same horrible trap that I fell into.

23

. . . how to make the decision whether or not to get married

The fact is that many people are not spiritually, emotionally, and / or financially ready to get married. Many people make the decision way too quickly. A quick decision is often a bad decision.

The decision to get married is a monumental decision in your life. It is the most important decision that you will ever make, except for your decision to become a Christian.

Whenever you make any type of important decision, you need to take it to God in prayer repeatedly. You need to ask Him for wisdom and guidance. This is especially true when considering marriage. You need to talk to God about the decision over a long period of time (months, if not longer). You need to take time to listen to God speaking to you during your prayer time and you also need to read your Bible on a regular basis (1 Corinthians is a good book to read when you are considering marriage).

Please ask God and yourself questions like:

- Has the person who you are considering marrying demonstrated, without a doubt, that they are a fully devoted follower of Christ?

- Are you, without a doubt, a fully devoted follower of Christ?

- Will marrying you help the other person draw closer to Christ?

- Will marrying the other person help you to draw closer to Christ?

- Has Christ been at the head of your dating relationship?

- Will Christ be at the head of your marriage?

- Are you willing to make a lifelong commitment, no matter what, to the other person?

- Is the other person willing to make a lifelong commitment, no matter what, to you?

- Are you both willing to agree that divorce is not even an option, no matter what?

- Are you trustworthy?

- Has the other person proven that they are trustworthy?

- Do both of you know how to control your money?

- Do both of you have at least two years of work experience, after completing your education, under your belt? (Please see Chapter 16.)

- Am I or is he or she too selfish to be married? (Marriage requires putting the other person first most of the time - which is a shock to many people - please see Chapter 26.)

- Do both of you have the same definition of what real love is?

- Do both of you have good communication / conflict resolution skills?

- Have you had experience in your dating relationship resolving conflicts in a constructive way?

- Have both of you shown the willingness and the ability to forgive each other? (people in a marriage relationship need to be able to forgive each other on a daily basis)

- Are you ignoring any of the danger signs mentioned in Chapter 20?

- Have you both decided to accept each other as you are - instead of trying to change the other person?

- If you are blessed with children, is one of you willing to stay home, especially through the preschool years, to meet their needs? Do you have a financial plan to be able to do so? (Please see Chapter 24.)

- Has your dating relationship been pleasing to God?

- Would your marriage be pleasing to God?

- Have you attended in-depth Christian premarital counseling with a qualified Pastor / Counselor?

As you can see there are many questions that need to be prayerfully answered.

It is also a very good idea to seek the counsel of Christian relatives and friends. If the majority of your Christian relatives and friends are opposed to your getting married, it is more than likely best to decide not to get married, or at the very least postpone the decision. There is no reason to rush into what could be a bad decision. If he or she is unhappy that you need more time to decide, it could be a danger sign - remember the verse in the Bible that says "Love is patient."

24

. . . children needing their parents

Odds are if you get married that you will one day be blessed with a child or children. A big problem that we have in society today is that the needs of children are secondary to the needs of adults. This means that many children are being shortchanged. They are not having their needs fulfilled by the people who can do it best - their parents. Instead the children are being sent off to some form of day care while their parents go off to work. From what I have read, large day care centers are one of the worst places for a child in terms of their emotional development.

I've heard lots of excuses like: "I need to work in order to make ends meet", "Both of us need to work in order for us to afford a house", "I won't be fulfilled without a career", etc. The fact is that children need one of their parents full-time during the preschool years, at the very least.

For the sake of your child or children, please develop a plan before you get married to make this possible. Keep in mind that no one can smile back at a child the way a parent can, no one can be more joyous at a child's first step than a parent can, no one can give a preschool child the loving discipline they need better than a parent can, and no one can love a child the way a parent can. Children need their parents.

James Wegert

25

. . . two dangerous attitudes

I used to have the "divorce won't happen to me" attitude. Never in my wildest dreams did I ever imagine being divorced in my lifetime. After all, I came from a good family with parents committed to each other, I was a Christian, I tried to be a nice person, I tried to meet her needs, and I thought we loved each other. Even when things got rough, I told myself that everything was going to be all right because we loved each other.

Unfortunately, my first marriage still ended in divorce. The problem was that at the time of our marriage neither she nor I was a fully devoted follower of Christ and we had different definitions of real love.

The truth is that the "divorce won't happen to me" attitude is dangerous because it can cause you to make bad decisions and it can lull you into complacency. A lifelong loving Christian marriage takes two people deeply committed to each other, a willingness to grow up (ouch) - as well as a lot of hard work, love, and forgiveness.

Another dangerous attitude is "divorce is no big deal." Please don't let seeing "celebrities" go through one divorce after another fool you into thinking that divorce is no big deal. It is a big deal for almost everyone who gets divorced. It is a big deal for your children - their lives will never be the same. Sadly, if you become divorced, it will affect you, your children, and your grandchildren in a negative way throughout your lives.

People who have the "divorce is no big deal" attitude are less likely to carefully go through the decision making process described in Chapter 23 and are more likely to make a bad marriage decision.

26

. . . the number one sin that we have to battle daily – Selfishness

We are naturally selfish - we are concerned about having good food in our belly, nice clothes on our back, a solid roof over our heads, and we want to feel important. However, too much selfishness is destructive to yourself and to your relationships with others. Face it, we live in a "Me First" society - people want what they want when they want it. This is exactly the opposite of how God wants us to live. He actually wants us to forget about our self and focus on loving others. Loving others (as well as loving God) will help you to have the best possible life here on earth. Contrary to popular belief, selfishness does not lead to long term happiness - "no baloney".

Whether we are single or married, we need to realize that the number one sin that we are going to have to battle on a daily basis is selfishness. We go through most of our single life with ourselves as our #1 concern. If we get married, all of a sudden after a few words said by a clergyman, someone else that we love is supposed to be our #1 concern. We are now #2. (If God blesses you with children, we become an even lower priority.) When we get married, we make a vow (promise) to God to love, honor, and cherish our lifelong mate regardless of whether we feel like doing it and regardless of what we receive in return.

To many people who get married, having to put someone else first is a big shock - it means that they can no longer say or do whatever they want, whenever they want. Old habits are often slow to die. It means that they have to grow up (sorry if this sounds insulting). I have to confess that there are times when I resent having to put my wife first and sometimes I fail to put her first. I have to ask God to forgive me for the resentment / failures and to help me focus on my daily commitment - loving my wife in a manner that is pleasing to God.

So, "How do you go about battling selfishness on a daily basis?" Regardless of what sin we are battling, it is always best to turn to our source of strength - God. We need to pray everyday asking for help and strength in our battle against selfishness. I realize that everyday seems like a bit much - but we need to realize that selfishness is a sin that we will battle daily throughout our lives.

(We've come up with a corny but fun way in our family to help people to recognize selfishness. When someone says something that is just out and out selfish - some of the other people say "goy!" in a somewhat long loud goofy manner. Goy! stands for "get off yourself." At first my boys thought it was corny (my wife still does), but now they think it's kind of fun. So when someone is bragging, we give him or her a "goy!" When someone is demanding their own way, we give them a "goy!" It has helped people in our family in a positive way to recognize when they are being selfish. Talk it over with your parents and see if they want to try it in your family.)

27

. . . the five main causes of divorce

The following are the main causes of divorce, in my opinion:

1. Not being and / or not being married to a fully devoted follower of Christ (Please see Chapter 12-15.)

2. Selfishness - which often shows itself through an unwillingness to put the needs of your spouse first, an unwillingness to control your tongue, and an unwillingness to grow up (Please see Chapter 26.)

3. Poor Communication and Conflict Resolution Skills - many people need to learn how to communicate well and how to resolve conflicts in a way that does not damage the relationship (communication and conflict resolution training should be part of the pre-marriage counseling curriculum of anyone who is considering marriage)

4. One or both of the spouses being unable or unwilling to control money (Please see Chapter 16.)

5. The husband and / or the wife not knowing what real love is (Please see Chapter 21.)

James Wegert

Epilogue

. . . be part of a revolution

We need a cultural revolution in order to help significantly reduce the divorce rate in our society that has reached epidemic proportions. For your sake, for the sake of your future children, and for the sake our society - we need to turn away from the existing culture of teen dating and turn to God instead.

I am proposing that teenagers spend the majority of their teenage years developing a close relationship with Jesus Christ, instead of spending too much of their precious time developing relationships with members of the opposite sex. I am proposing that teens not date one-on-one until they graduate from high school. Unfortunately, an epidemic needs strong medicine.

Before you get yourself too worked up, please hear me out. Here's what the cultural revolution would look like when it's achieved:

A dramatic increase in the. . .

- . . . number of teens who are fully devoted followers of Christ

- . . . amount of time that teens spend developing their relationship with Jesus Christ

- . . . number of teens waiting until they are a fully devoted follower of Christ before they date

. . . number of teen fully devoted followers of Christ who will only date other fully devoted followers of Christ

. . . number of teenagers, age sixteen and up, participating in group dating

. . . number of wholesome and fun recreational activities available for non-dating teens / group dating teens on Friday and Saturday nights

. . . number of people in a lifelong loving Christian marriage relationship

A dramatic decrease in the. . .

. . . number of teens who are participating in one-on-one dating

. . . number of teens with sexually transmitted diseases (The current numbers are absolutely shocking - sexually active teens don't seem to realize or don't seem to care that they are taking a very high risk of destroying their health. Unfortunately, some diseases can cause cancer or cause females to be infertile. Some diseases can never be cured. Please see p. 113.)

. . . divorce rate

In order to make this cultural revolution possible, we must find a way for churches, the "Y's", other Christian organizations, and recreation departments to provide wholesome and fun recreational activities for non-dating teens / group dating teens right up until curfew on Friday and Saturday nights.

We must provide teens with wholesome and fun alternatives to one-on-one dating if we hope to dramatically reduce the divorce rate.

Here are recommendations for how to make this cultural revolution happen:

- Thoroughly educate teens about dating and about the dangers of sexually transmitted diseases

- Ask parents not to allow their teens below age sixteen to date under any circumstances (as you read in Chapter 11 - the later the better)

- Ask parents to strongly encourage their teen to become a fully devoted follower of Christ before they date and to date only another fully devoted follower of Christ

- Ask parents to allow only group dating, with three or more couples, by their teens in high school. Time alone needs to be eliminated.

- Ask parents to allow their high school teens to only date someone who is no more than two grade levels higher than their teen's grade level (for example, a sophomore could date no higher than a senior - a junior could date no higher than a freshman in college, etc.)

- Ask parents to allow only group dating with three or more couples even if the person their teen is dating has graduated from high school. (The purpose of this recommendation is to protect teens from being taking advantage of by smooth talking young adults.)

- Ask parents to allow their teens to date one-on-one only after they have graduated from high school

- Ask churches to make developing youth into fully devoted followers of Christ their #1 priority

- Ask churches to budget the funds needed to achieve this priority

- Ask churches, the "Y's", other Christian organizations, and recreation departments to provide wholesome and fun recreational activities right up until curfew for non-dating teens / group dating teens on Friday and Saturday nights.

Your reaction to the proposed revolution may be, "It's not going to happen, that's impossible!" Please remember Mark, chapter 10, verse 27 that says, "all things" are possible with God.

I invite you to consider being part of a revolution!

(Please don't forget to read the Final Word to both Girls and Guys, Final Word to Girls, and the Final Word to Guys on p. 81-86.)

Final Word to both Girls and Guys

The lives of more and more teenagers are spinning out of control. It's hard to believe that so many teenagers around the world are dating at an early age and are giving their bodies before marriage to someone else for fun, because they think they love someone, because they think someone loves them, or because they hope they will be loved if they do so. (I read an article in the newspaper today that said about 34 percent of women in America become pregnant before the age of 20 . . . what a sad statistic for the women, but even more so for the children - many of whom will grow up without a constant strong loving father figure in their life.)

Many teenagers move from one relationship to another searching for real love. They don't realize that they are looking for love in all the wrong places. They don't realize that they are damaging their emotions (Please see Chapter 10.). They don't realize that they are setting themselves up for a wide variety of life changing events such as:

- getting a sexually transmitted disease** (It's not a joke, it's a horrible epidemic - why do you think there are commercials on TV advertising a drug that can help to control outbreaks of Herpes, a sexually transmitted disease for which there is no cure? - why do you think the cases of cervical cancer and infertility in women are skyrocketing? Please see the list of highly recommended reading on p. 113.)

- becoming a Mother without being married**

- becoming a Father without being married**
- realizing that the person who you gave your body to doesn't love you - in fact they don't even know what real love is**

- realizing that you don't love the person that you have given your body to**

- an unloving marriage relationship

- Divorce**

**Please remember that Jesus Christ loves you unconditionally. As long as you are alive it is not too late to turn to Him, ask for forgiveness (regardless of what you have done), trust in Christ alone as your Savior, and start living your life for Him! (Please see Chapter 5 and Chapter 12 for more information.)

(Please see the Final Word to Girls on p. 83 and the Final Word to Guys on p. 85.)

Final Word to Girls

I hope that this book has succeeded in giving you a perspective on teen dating that you have never heard before.

Here's a few final words and it's going to sound blunt (sorry): You need to know that many men are selfish / immature and they want to use your body for their pleasure. Many will tell you almost anything (the most effective being "I love you") in order to get what they want. I realize that no one likes to be told to "wake up", but you need to "wake up" to these facts if you haven't done so already.

Another thing that you need to know is that unfortunately good men are few and far between - and that a big part of the reason for this is that women's standards for who is acceptable dating material is not high enough. It seems that many women are willing to date almost anyone. (In contrast, God wants you to be very selective about whom you date because He truly loves you and wants only the very best for you.) Quite frankly, you need to know that dating the wrong man can ruin your life. Contrary to popular belief, it's better to be a lonely old maid than to be married to the wrong man. (Please see Chapter 11-17 for information about when and who to date.)

If women are strong and have high standards - this will help to force men to grow up. It's not easy being God's woman in this world - but he will bless your life if you live your life for Him!

I hope that reading this book will help you to have high standards for yourself and for the person that you decide to date.

Blessings,

Mr. W.

PS Please don't forget to see the information about Teen U™, the Teen U™ website, and the list of highly recommended reading list on p. 87-114. We encourage you to submit a question about teen dating (first names and initials are changed to protect your privacy) at www.TeenU.net. Thanks!

Final Word to Guys

(If you read the "Final word to Girls", this is going to sound very familiar.)

I hope that this book has succeeded in giving you a perspective on teen dating that you have never heard before.

Here's a few final words and it's going to sound blunt (sorry): You need to know that many women are selfish / immature and they desperately want someone to love them - someone to meet their emotional and other needs. Many will tell you almost anything (the most effective being "I love you") and are willing to give you their bodies before marriage in order to get what they want. I realize that no one likes to be told to "wake up," but you need to "wake up" to these facts before you fall into their trap.

Another thing you need to know is that unfortunately good woman are few and far between - and that a big part of the reason for this is that men's standards for who is acceptable dating material is not high enough. It seems that many men are willing to date almost anyone. (In contrast, God wants you to be very selective about whom you date because He truly loves you and wants only the very best for you. The Bible says in the book of Proverbs, chapter 31, verse 10 that a good wife is a precious treasure.)

Quite frankly, you need to know that dating the wrong woman can ruin your life. Even just one date can lead to disaster. I know that sounds hard to believe - but it's true, here's how:

some women are so attractive on the outside that you completely forget that beauty on the inside is what you should be looking for - and sadly you end up marrying the wrong person. (Please see Chapter 11-17 for information about when and who to date.)

If men are strong and have high standards - this will help to force women to grow up. It's not easy being God's man in this world - but he will bless your life if you live your life for Him!

I hope that reading this book will help you to have high standards for yourself and for the person that you decide to date.

Blessings,

Mr. W.

PS Please don't forget to see the information about Teen U™, the Teen U™ website, and the list of highly recommended reading on p. 87-114. We encourage you to submit a question about teen dating (first names and initials are changed to protect your privacy) at www.TeenU.net. Thanks!

Appendix: Information about Teen U™, the Teen U™ website (www.TeenU.net), and a list of highly recommended reading

(The following pages are a sample of what can be found at www.TeenU.net – please check it out!)

Teen U™

...Be Free   John 8:32

It seems that regardless of our age, pre-teens to senior citizens, many of us seem to think that we know it all and that we don't need any education about dating, personal finances, preparing for marriage, marriage, parenting, etc. The truth is that regardless of our age and our experience – we don't know it all. You may have heard the saying, "It's always a good idea to learn from other people's mistakes – because you don't have time to make them all yourself." You may be thinking, "Why in the world do I need all this education?" Our response is – now is the time to learn before you make a life changing mistake. Why not learn from other people's mistakes now in order to maximize the possibility that you will have a lifelong loving Christian marriage relationship and to minimize the possibility of going through a devastating divorce in the future?

Q.

What is the mission of Teen U™?

A.

To help people to have lifelong loving Christian marriage relationships and to reduce the divorce rate in our society

Q.

Why was Teen U™ started?

A.

Teen U™ was started to achieve its mission (please see the previous question). It hopes to achieve the mission by making good information with "no baloney" available to pre-teens / teens, by helping churches to meet the needs of teens, and by advocating that wholesome and fun teen recreational activities be made available every Friday and Saturday night at a reasonable cost.

Q.

How is Teen U™ organized?

A.

Teen U™ offers five courses: Dating, Personal Finances, Preparing for Marriage, Marriage, and Parenting. A course is completed by reading the required book and taking a written test. The book *Straight Talk About Teen Dating* is available through Booklocker.com. Other required books are available from bookstores and / or the web. A set of tests for the five courses can be purchased through the www.TeenU.net website or by using the order form on p. 95 of this book. Quantity and friend referral

discounts are available. A Teen U™ graduate
T-shirt is sent to the graduate (at no
additional fee) when the tests for all five
courses have been passed.

The website of Teen U™ (www.TeenU.net),
also gives pre-teens and teens a forum to
ask questions about teen dating**. Some
questions and answers (with names changed
to protect your privacy and the innocent) are
posted on the website with the hope that
reading answers to real life questions may be
helpful to teens. We regret that we are
unable to post answers to all of the
questions submitted.

**Please be aware that the answers to these
questions are <u>not</u> written by licensed
counselors.

How to order the book – *Straight Talk About Teen Dating*

You may order the book *Straight Talk About Teen Dating* at www.Booklocker.com. Quantity discounts are available – please go to www.Booklocker.com for details.

How to order the tests required to become a Teen U™ graduate:

You may order the set of five tests for all of the Teen U™ courses by completing the Test order form on p. 95 (please note the 25%

discount on the tests for referring your friends!) and mailing it to:

> Teen U
> PO Box 5234
> Lancaster, PA 17606-5234

The fee for one copy of the set of five tests is $16 – including all shipping and handling.

The fee includes test scoring and a Teen U™ Graduate T-shirt (the T-shirt will be sent to you after you pass all five tests).

(Quantity discounts for tests are available – please go to www.TeenU.net for details)

James Wegert

Test order form:

_____ set(s) of tests @ $16

= _____ Subtotal(1)

Please calculate your discount if you have decided to refer your friends to Teen U™ (please see the Friend Referral form on p. 97):

(1) x .25 (25%) _____ = Amount of discount(2)

_____Total amount due (1)–(2)

Please make your check or money order payable to Teen U. Thank you!

Your First Name_____

Last Initial (only)_____

Address_____

State_____Zip_____

(Quantity discounts for tests are available –
please go to www.TeenU.net for details.)

Friend Referral:

_____Yes, I would like my friends to know about Teen U™. We will send your friends an e-mail once a month telling them information about Teen U™, a copy of a question and answer from our online forum about teen dating, or possibly a short excerpt from the book *Straight Talk About Teen Dating*. Your name will not be included in the e-mail. It will just say something like "a friend thought you might be interested in this information." (The e-mail addresses of your friends will not be shared with anyone else!)

(Please print!)

Friend #1
e-mail address:_____

Friend #2
e-mail address:_____

Friend #3
e-mail address:_____

Friend #4
e-mail address:_____

Friend #5
e-mail address:_____

Your First name_____

Last initial (only)_____

Your e-mail address (if you would like the
same monthly Teen U™ information that will
be sent to your friends and occasional

special e-mails from Teen U™)

_____ (never shared!)

Help spread the word about Teen U™!

If you would like to help us achieve our mission by spreading the word about Teen U™ after you have read the book *Straight Talk About Teen Dating* – you can do so by wearing a Teen U™ T-shirt, by putting a Teen U™ static sticker in the rear window of your vehicle, by giving static stickers to your friends who are willing to display them, and by referring friends to receive Teen U™ e-mails. If you are willing to help, please let us know by completing the "Yes, I'll Help" form on p. 103, and mailing it to us at:

Teen U
PO Box 5234
Lancaster, PA 17606-5234

We will send you a nice FREE T-shirt that says Teen U™ on the front and:

Got questions
about Teen Dating?™
www.TeenU.net

or

...Be Free™
www.TeenU.net

or another Teen U™ slogan the back. (shirt colors, styles, and wording may vary)

We will also send you free static stickers for the back windows of vehicles.

James Wegert

"Yes I'll Help" Form

_____Yes, I've read the book *Straight Talk About Teen Dating* and I'd like to help spread the word about Teen U™!**.

_____Yes, I'm willing to spread the word about Teen U™ by wearing a Teen U™ T-shirt at least once a month in public (school, the mall, amusement park, etc.) Size (please circle) adult small, adult medium, adult large, adult extra large.

_____Yes, I'm willing to display a static sticker in the rear window of our vehicle and ask some of my friends to do the same. Please send me _____stickers. (Please do not request more than you can use. Thanks!)

_____Yes, I'm willing to provide Teen U™ with the e-mail addresses of some of my friends.

(Additional e-mail addresses do not have to be provided if you have already completed a Friend Referral form – unless you have more friends that you would like to know about Teen U™!) We will send your friends an e-mail once a month telling them information about Teen U™, a copy of a question and answer from our online forum about teen dating, or possibly a short excerpt from the book *Straight Talk About Teen Dating*. Your name will not be included in the e-mail. It will just say something like "a friend thought you might be interested in this information." (The e-mail addresses of your friends will not be shared with anyone else!)

_____I have already completed a FRIEND REFERRAL form

(Please print!)

Friend #1
e-mail address:_____

Friend #2
e-mail address:_____

Friend #3
e-mail address:_____

Friend #4
e-mail address:_____

Friend #5
e-mail address:_____

Your First Name_____

Last Initial (only)_____

Address_____

State_____Zip_____

(We need this mailing address in order to mail the T-shirt and the static stickers. It will not be shared!)

Your e-mail address (if you would like the same monthly Teen U™ information that will be sent to your friends and occasional special e-mails from Teen U™)

_____ (never shared!)

**Please e-mail us by clicking on the Contact Us tab at www.TeenU.net with your comments about the book *Straight Talk About Teen Dating* as well as your suggestions for additional chapters, improvement, etc.

Your comments may appear on the Testimonials page of the website (your first name and last initial will be changed to protect your privacy). Your suggestions may be used to improve future editions of the book. Thanks!

James Wegert

Teen U™ Courses:

1. Dating

Required Book: *Straight Talk About Teen Dating* by James Wegert

Comment: "The information in this book can help you to have a lifelong loving Christian marriage and eternal life!"

2. Personal Finances

Required Book: *Complete Idiot's Guide to Money for Teens* by Susan Shelley*

Comment: "Learning how to control your finances when you are young can really pay!"

3. Preparing for Marriage

Required Book: *Preparing for Marriage: A Guide for Christian Couples* by Donald Luther*

Comment: "Now is the time to start preparing if God wants you to be married in the future. You don't have to be in a dating relationship in order to learn from this book."

4. Marriage

Required Book: *The Five Love Languages* by Gary Chapman*

Comment: "This book will help you to find out the needs and meet the needs of your husband / wife if you are married in the future."

5. <u>Parenting</u>

Required book: *Systematic Training for Effective Parenting* by Don Dinkmeyer Sr., Gary McKay, and Don Dinkmeyer Jr.*

Comment: "Before you are a Mom or a Dad is a great time to learn how to be a firm, fair, kind, and consistent parent."

James Wegert

Highly recommended reading:

Sex Has A Price Tag by Pam Stenzel
with Crystal Kirgiss* (This book contains
crucial information that you need to know
about sexually transmitted diseases – it can
literally save your life!)

Group Dating: 301 Ideas by Blair Tolman,
Tristan Toman, and Kelli Weaver* (This book
can spark your imagination for wholesome
and fun group dating activities.)

*Teen U™ is not affiliated with any of
these books or authors.

Do you have a suggestion for a course
that you feel Teen U™ should be offering?
Do you have any suggestions for improving
the Teen U™ website? If so, please click on

the Contact Us tab us at www.TeenU.net to let us know. Thanks!